The Will to Win

Reginald Lee

authorHOUSE®

AuthorHouse™
1663 Liberty Drive
Bloomington, IN 47403
www.authorhouse.com
Phone: 1 (800) 839-8640

Published by AuthorHouse 06/26/2015

ISBN: 978-1-4969-7183-8 (sc)
ISBN: 978-1-4969-7182-1 (e)

Library of Congress Control Number: 2015903005

Print information available on the last page.

Any people depicted in stock imagery provided by Thinkstock are models, and such images are being used for illustrative purposes only.
Certain stock imagery © Thinkstock.

This book is printed on acid-free paper.

Contents

Sports teach you to mature as a player and person. The most important game you'll play is the game of life. I've broken down how to win and what it takes to win into pertinent details. The book will benefit coaches, players, and fans. This book will show a player that, in order to be successful, he has to be more than a good athlete. He has to be a student of the game. A player who understands the mental side of the game has a distinct advantage over his opponent. Winning is an art and a skill.

Energy, passion, and the love of the game all translate into the will to win. The will to win is about heart, soul, and character. There is nothing stronger than willpower. The will to win is psychological warfare, where the players with the most desire and passion for the game come out on top. There is no *quit* in the word *team*. Where there is desire and commitment, there will be results. The will to win is the mental game within the game. Ask for no mercy and show none! All champions have one thing in common, the will to win.

Winning starts with a philosophy. Cultivating a winning attitude is a need to succeed. Successful teams resemble each other. A team must have a good self-image and no self-doubt. A good coach and a good environment add up to a winning tradition. A winning team has confidence and swagger. A winning attitude is contagious. Every team needs a combination to succeed. That combination includes power, speed, youth, and experience. Victories are easy when everybody does his job. When a team controls the tempo, they control their own fate. Turn anger into intensity! Winning gives a team a feeling of exhilaration and pride. Expectations will evolve into excitement. Winning teaches a team how to come together for a common goal and purpose.

Motivation

Motivation is emotional energy. It is the internal desire to be the best. Motivation is making others believe what you do. Motivation is recognizing a sense of urgency. Motivation is looking forward to a challenge. Motivation is when your instincts, emotions, and intensity naturally take over. Motivation is a mental rebirth. It is when certain words inspire action. When a player is motivated, he becomes more focused.

The objective in developing a will to win is to get better, stronger, and wiser with each victory. Every game takes as much mental preparation as it does physical preparation.

Life is a marathon. Set a precedent, and live by it.

A Legend

A legend is a special breed of athlete with the ability and desire to take his game to the next level. A legend is a beloved hero and a quintessential professional. A legend is a player that has an unparalleled career, raises the bar, transcends a sport, and becomes a cultural icon. The legacy of a legend grows with time.

A legend is an embodiment of history and a model of consistency. A legend changes the game and does things that no one else has ever done. A legend sets standards for others to follow. A legend leaves an indelible mark on a sport. A legend changes the way we define greatness.

Dynasty

Teams build a dynasty when they display unmatched excellence—the ability to dominate a sport over several seasons. Building a dynasty is about taking success to the next level. A team must win several championships to be considered a dynasty. Dynasties usually have legendary coaches. Dynasties have hall-of-fame players who redefine their positions and a team that redefines an era. The balance of power shifts to one team, one that has assembled more talent than any other. A dynasty is a team that plays the game nearly to perfection and capitalizes on all their opponents' mental mistakes.

Dynasties have superstars that are in their prime. The core of the team must remain intact. Dynasties win close games. They don't feel the pressure! Dynasties play loose and with swagger. Dynasties are aware of their place in history long before history is written. Dynasties are feared and respected. Dynasties are an institution and a model for other teams to copy.

Sports in College

The college game is about the essence of what is right. Players are constantly trying to prove themselves. The college game builds character. The college game is about young adults trying to find maturity. The college game will always have more passion than the pro game.

The college game has more rivalries, more intensity, and less complacency. It inspires more loyalty from fans. The college game is played with more enthusiasm and emotion. The college game is about tradition and pride. In college, the rules are more team-oriented. College coaches do more teaching. The college game is about substance, not style. College athletes learn about camaraderie and exactly what they can accomplish through teamwork.

Competitors

Hard work and intensity give an athlete a competitive edge. Competitors like to compete. They want to win. They expect to win. They play to win. There's no such thing as a moral victory. Competition pits one person's fortitude against another's.

Losing hurts! Competitors take losing personally. They are constantly looking for ways to redeem themselves. A competitor feeds off emotions and wants to atone for every loss and every mistake. A competitor never gives up on any play.

How do you recognize a competitor? A competitor is a warrior that thrives on pressure. He is the last person to leave the building after practice. He is constantly practicing fundamentals, lifting weights, and studying game film. That competitive spirit makes certain players special.

A competitor willingly responds to a challenge. He always gives his all. In his heart, he knows that he's a winner. He always comes through when it counts. A competitor never lacks in confidence.

All a competitor needs is an opportunity. A competitor knows no limits and concedes nothing.

A competitor doesn't need any extra incentives. To a competitor, every game is a big game. Not only does a competitor want to win, he wants to dominate.

The skills that you need for success in sports are the same ones that you need for success in life. They include the following: discipline, self-esteem, leadership, patience, instincts, a good attitude, maturity, responsibility, desire, confidence, mental toughness, hard work/practice, character, intuitiveness, and motivation.

Game Plans

Game plans should be tested and refined. The success of the game plan isn't so much strategy as it is execution and preparation. Your team needs to prepare, practice, and work harder than the other team. Any system takes time, experience, maturity, and the right personnel to oversee its execution. If the players believe in the system, the system will succeed. When players don't know the offensive or defensive scheme, they play tentatively.

A team has to establish momentum and have playoff savvy. A team must be consistent from week to week and play to play. If a team prepares and studies well, it will play well. The coach should have a game plan and list of adjustments. Players have to set aside personal goals, conflicts, and stats. The main objective is to win each game.

Play Callers

Play callers have to be bold. They can't be tentative. Players can sense when the play caller is being too conservative. Tentativeness will be interpreted as a lack of trust. Play callers can't be predictable. Play callers have to embrace new technology that will help them measure tendencies.

If your team has had a long layoff, you should script the first few plays and make sure they are executed properly. This will help the offense gain rhythm. Methodological offenses are the best and most consistent. Methodological offenses systematically execute one play at a time.

When an offense is stagnant, get the ball in the hands of your leader and best player. Moreover, a balanced offense lifts the spirit of the entire team because it allows everyone to get involved.

Sportsmanship

Sportsmanship is about protecting the integrity of the game. With sportsmanship, you gain credibility and respect. Play hard and within the rules! Sportsmanship is the mark of mutual respect between opponents. Sportsmanship is about putting what's right ahead of winning.

Sportsmanship is an attitude. It is about being a gentleman first and an athlete second. Sportsmanship means winning and losing with class. Don't brag and don't complain. Just play the game the right way.

Sportsmanship involves the following: shaking hands, having self-control and composure, setting principles and standards, being responsible for your actions, knowing that winning is the goal but winning isn't everything, being a role model, having an unselfish attitude and respect for your sport and the people in it, playing by the rules, having a code of conduct and team discipline, possessing maturity, and being involved in the community.

Defeatism

Losing can be summed up in two words: *missed opportunities*. The only way to change a losing attitude is to win. Stop complaining about officials, and play the game! During a losing streak, a coach finds out the character of his team. A losing attitude has a domino effect. It will send a team into a downward spiral. Therefore, a player's mind-set after a loss is very important. When you start to accept losing, it becomes a habit. Losing should never enter your thought process. There's a difference between losing and being a loser.

Bad teams find ways and reasons to lose. Bad teams wait for bad things to happen. They often self-destruct. Good teams are able to put tough losses behind them and focus on the next game.

Losing teams usually create bad habits that are hard to get rid of. A team loses a big lead when its members lose their focus and concentration. A team goes on a losing streak when its role players don't know their roles. Only losing teams make excuses. Moral victories are for losing teams.

Another reason for losing streaks is that the team is playing aimlessly, that is, without a purpose. Its members lack focus and discipline, and the team is not fundamentally sound.

After a loss, the team has to bounce back emotionally and psychologically and must change what it's doing or get better at what it's already doing. The team must look within and has to regain its focus and confidence.

After a loss, go back and practice the fundamentals. The practice will be more intense. There will be a sense of urgency. Losing creates doubt in the locker room.

Refocusing

Develop a positive mental attitude! A player should go back to doing the things he has been doing right and concentrate on the fundamentals. After playing against a rival, there is strong potential for a letdown in the next game because the team is so emotional. When a player starts to refocus, he eliminates mental mistakes. A player has to be able to think clearly when the adrenaline is flowing.

Remember that, no matter what happens during the game, the main goal is to win. You have enough on your mind trying to defeat your opponent. Don't defeat yourself as well. It is imperative that you stay focused. When you lose your mental focus, you lose your edge and your intensity.

Refocusing is about putting all your energy in the proper place. Let your energy work for you, not against you! Refocusing involves re-creating a sense of urgency. In order to remain focused, a player has to stay humble. Refocusing is mentally eliminating fatigue and gaining a certain level of confidence.

When things start at a slow pace, we tend to change our perceptions of ourselves. You must keep your focus. When you are focused, you're able to communicate better with your teammates. Being focused is being mentally locked in.

Being focused is important because mental errors often keep a good player from being great. Focus is the highest level of concentration. Focus is awareness, being ready all the time and getting into a zone. Being focused is about taking one play at a time. A player's focus has to be greater than the pressure. There are two sides to being focused: your memory of what just happened and your anticipation of what's going to happen. If a team leader isn't focused, the rest of the team won't be focused. The team leader must lead by example when it comes to being focused. Being focused shows that a player is willing to be accountable on every play. The more focused that a player becomes, the less pressure that he will feel.

Chemistry

There must be a mutual respect or chemistry among teammates. Chemistry is when different personalities, skills, and talent complement each other. Teams are mainly inconsistent because they lack chemistry. Team chemistry is believing in each other during the good and bad times. Team chemistry is helping and encouraging each other. A team has chemistry when the players form an immediate bond. The best way to develop team chemistry is with veteran leadership. Sometimes losing a superstar can bring a team closer. Chemistry is when players emotionally and mentally come together. Chemistry is where a team gets its identity.

Chemistry is a group of players who share the same passion for the game. Not only is a player just playing for himself, he's also playing for the guy next to him. Chemistry is putting the team ahead of the individual. Chemistry is where the concept of team is transformed to reality. For chemistry to develop, leadership has to set a tone and show unselfishness. Chemistry is everyone moving together in the same direction. Chemistry is when a player uses the lessons and his experience he has had with his teammates to bond closer together.

Chemistry is togetherness on the team bus and outside the arena, not just during the games. Chemistry is having your teammate's back. Chemistry is believing, caring, supporting, and rooting for each other. Chemistry is having confidence in your teammates. Chemistry is everyone playing together at a high level. Chemistry is when a group of players like each other and they like playing together. Chemistry is excitement and good energy among teammates. Chemistry is coming together and jelling together. The entire team should give high-fives after a good play, not just half the team. Chemistry is staying together as a group and remaining poised when faced with adversity. When one player is hurting, everyone is hurting.

Destiny

Destiny is the maximum level that your skills will take you. Greatness is perceived and then achieved.

Tradition and memories can only carry a team so far. Tradition is more than just a legacy. It's a standard that an organization sets. History and desire usually add up to success. History isn't made during the season. It's made at the end of it.

Discipline

Discipline is the force that directs your actions. You can't accomplish anything in life without discipline. Discipline comes from mental toughness, pride, and a desire for inner perfection. Discipline is the first step toward dedication. It is being organized, having a plan, developing a work ethic, being focused on details and prepared, controlling aggression, being committed, and showing maturity. Discipline helps to promote a stable environment. If something isn't done right, go back and do it again. Discipline helps to prevent complacency. Discipline is when everything you do has a purpose.

Playing with discipline means playing within the game plan and not beating yourself A player's discipline is tested the most when he's tired. When a player is fatigued, he still has to trust his training and fundamentals.

There is a thin line between winning and losing. That line is called discipline.
R. E. Lee

Undisciplined Teams

Undisciplined teams commit silly penalties and fouls. They get caught out of position. They can't finish the game and have no killer instincts. They don't study their playbooks or opponent's tendencies. They don't play within the framework of the system. They play lazy on defense.

The Perfect Player

The perfect player has mental game day toughness. He is team-oriented and self-motivated. He is humble and has a positive attitude. He is a class act on and off the field. He plays physical with intensity. He has good character and is a devoted family man. He is fundamentally sound and has a great work ethic. He is a born athlete and a motivator on the field.

Versatility

Versatility gives the defense more to think about. Versatility puts relentless pressure on a defense. Versatility can offset the importance of depth because a coach has players who can fill so many roles without substituting. Versatility gives a team flexibility regardless of the position. Versatility has saved the careers of many veteran players. Good defensive and championship teams always have several versatile players.

Versatile players must be physically and mentally dedicated. They must be in shape and be able to handle several different responsibilities. In the era of the salary cap, versatility is extremely important. Versatility gives a coach the ability to change his defense and offense without changing the lineup. Versatility causes your opponent to constantly have to adjust. Versatility allows a team to overcome many mistakes and injuries.

Confidence

It doesn't matter what other people believe as long as you believe in yourself. You can't fake confidence. You either have it or don't. Confidence means not having to think. Just use your instincts. You just make things happen! Although confidence is shown externally, it comes from inside and from experience. Confidence gives you the momentum to keep moving forward. Confidence is stored in your memory just in case you have to confront the same situation again.

Confidence is just as important as the Xs and Os. The most fragile thing in the sports world is confidence. Don't get overwhelmed by any situation! Confidence is never questioning your own ability. Confidence is athletic arrogance. Confidence is knowing your best effort can beat your opponent's best effort. Confidence is not worrying about other people's expectations.

A player has to treat defeat as just another obstacle to overcome. He can't let defeat have a long-term effect on him mentally. Confidence is the only way to control fear. Confidence is a sense of belonging. It is a mental comfort zone. A champion knows his limits and can go beyond them. This is done with confidence.

Confidence is built quicker in a stable environment. Confidence is positive thinking and a positive attitude. Confidence comes from successful repetition. Confidence is a belief in yourself. That belief starts with hard work.

I never measure myself against anyone else. It's only against my own ability with no limitations. Confidence is trusting the work that I've done through practice.

Playing in a Mental Zone

Nothing can go wrong! No one can stop you. Everything is moving in slow motion. You can read and react before the defense can adjust. Objects appear larger! Nothing can break your concentration! You're feeling it, and your adrenaline is flowing. Your vision and your physical strength begin to increase. As the game goes on, you just get stronger. There are no signs of fatigue or slowing down. Your natural instincts take over.

Injuries

Face reality. The human body is prone to injuries. An injured player will need the full support of his family and friends. He should stay away from environments that lead to depression or people who offer too much sympathy. Sometimes, it is best for an injured player to temporarily disconnect from teammates.

A player will experience setbacks on the comeback trail. Injuries will make a player look at his career at a different perspective. Injuries will reduce a player's range of motion. Mentally, he has to regain his confidence. If a player loses his aggression, he'll never capture his old form or his elite status. A player never wants injuries to determine his fate. Injuries make for a smaller margin of error.

The timetable for recovering is different for every player. After surgery, a player should rest for several weeks before beginning rehab.

Next Man Up

Players work hard all season, and they have to be prepared for their opportunities. If someone goes down, the pressure falls on everyone else to step up. When a player is hurt, he has to come out of the lineup because it hard for him to adjust to the speed of the game. If a player isn't doing his job or if he's hurt and can't do his job, the next player will step up and do it. When a player is injured, it increases the opportunities for everyone else. The next superstar may be sitting on the bench, waiting for his opportunity.

Training Camp Goals

The goals of training camp is to evaluate young talent, form a cohesive and consistent unit, eliminate mental mistakes, stay injury-free, put new systems in place, get in shape, make players familiar with the team philosophy, define season objectives, set a tempo, and improve every day.

Attributes of a Potent Offense

Attributes of a potent offense include speed, power, balance, and discipline and patience. It attacks defensive weaknesses. It is prepared and in shape. It controls the tempo. It is diversified and creative. It makes quick adjustments and takes advantage of opportunities. It has rhythm and timing. It maintains focus and has intensity. It has chemistry and killer instinct.

Keys to a Potent Offense

A team can set the tempo with emotion, intensity, and energy. Find gaps in the zone defense and stretch the zone. The offense must be quicker and more physical than the defense. Attack a pressure defense to let your opponent know the team is not intimidated. Don't let a zone defense take away your aggressiveness! A team can't panic when they get behind. Match your best player up against a rookie.

A potent offense has good chemistry and flawless execution. When a team has the lead, stay with the game plan. If a team is going to make a mistake, make an aggressive mistake. A potent offense will never relax and has that killer instinct. Offensive plays work because of scouting reports and practice.

In a must-win situation, the team has to respond. Use veteran leadership to regroup after a loss. Don't just survive. Win outright! A balanced attack will find the weak spots in the defense. A balanced attack will keep the defense honest. The defense won't know exactly what to expect.

Against a multiple-option offense, the defense constantly has to adjust. One-dimensional teams don't win championships. A fast-paced offense physically and mentally wears down the opponent. If a team doesn't have an offensive identity, it won't be successful.

The Winning Philosophy

Winning builds confidence. Savor a victory for one day. There's no consolation in losing. A team is only as tough as its reputation. Don't let another team's tactics affect your approach to the game.

Winning on the road is a major accomplishment. It takes mental toughness. A team must have discipline and patience on the road. In a rematch, the team that lost the last time has all the motivation. Teamwork is what I call the winning combination.

Defining a Winner

How do you define a winner? Is it by wins or loses or by the way a team wins?

The answer: Winning is an attitude. It is about confidence and sportsmanship. The power of winning is inside of you, but you must find it. Winning is about desire. You have to prove something to yourself before you can prove it to someone else.

Potential

Potential is work in progress. It is the ability to change nothing into something. Coaches have to nurture potential and be patient. Potential is raw talent that needs to be developed. Potential in unpredictable. In the stock market, potential would be a junk bond. *Potential* is a word that has gotten a lot of coaches and general managers fired. Potential is unproven talent. Potential is a vision of things to come in the future.

The Myth

It is a myth that players learn by losing. They learn more by winning. However, failure can be used as an enemy or an ally. It is wise to use failure as a motivational tool.

Death and failure reminds us of our mortality. I don't think sports should reward teams for second place because people aren't rewarded for second place in life. If you're not competing to win, why compete?

Scouting

The most important part of an organization is scouting. Teams today have more scouts, and they pay them large salaries. Scouting has improved dramatically because of technology and the speed in which scouts can acquire information. However, scouts still can't measure a player's desire and determination.

Scouts should find out about any injury that a player has had in the past. Players should be measured from head to toe for muscles and body fat. Scouts emphasize size, strength, speed, ability, and potential.

When scouting, scouts want to study every aspect of a player's game and chart the information. A scout should talk to the player's family and friends to find out about the player's personality and habits. A scouting report is a report of opinions. It is a gut feeling about a player. A scouting report should describe how well a player handles pressure and fits into a system. Scouting is time-consuming and hard work. The purpose of a scouting report is to evaluate a player's strengths and weaknesses.

Scouting is not an exact science. It is an art and the most difficult job in sports. Don't randomly scout a player during any game! Scout a player when he is playing a tough opponent or another great player. This will show how well the player performs in big games and will give the scout a barometer to measure the athlete against.

The Playoffs

In the playoffs, the energy level increases, and the adrenaline is flowing. In the playoffs, the home team wins most of the games. That's why the home field advantage is so important. In a playoff rematch, the regular season loser has an advantage because of the motivation factor. The second game of the playoffs series is usually the most pivotal. In the playoffs, a team has to play every game like its back is against the wall. In a long series, both teams must make adjustments.

In the playoffs, the teams can throw out records and statistics. The playoffs are about heart, hard work, desire, and guts. A team should approach the playoffs with dedication, discipline, and sacrifice. In the playoffs, a team has to play with the same confidence it played with all season. Furthermore, a team has to be more aggressive during the playoffs.

A team has to come out with emotions and intensity. Don't be left thinking what could have been! Players can't make mental mistakes at this stage of the season. In the playoffs, a team can't rely solely on its stars. Someone else has to step it up.

To win in the playoffs, it takes more than talent. A team needs to have the intangibles. A team can't make mental mistakes, and it must play solid defense. Role players have to produce coming off the bench, and great players have to be selfish for once in their lives.

In the playoffs, a team sometimes has to go back home to find its identity. In the playoffs, there must be a sense of urgency and attention to details. In the playoffs, a team must maintain the same intensity of the road as it has at home. In the playoffs, teams rely on the intangibles, like momentum, confidence, preparation, and mental toughness. In the playoffs, a team wants to score early and then let its veteran leadership take over.

Mental Toughness

Mental toughness is the ability to bounce back from a mistake and make a big play. Pressure is an ally. It will help a player focus. A mentally tough player keeps grinding it out when he's hurt. Mental toughness is finishing what you have started. Mental toughness comes from pride and self-esteem. A mentally tough player doesn't cave in to steep expectations or become complacent after success. Concede nothing. Play hard until the end!

Mental toughness is contagious. Adversity can only affect a player if he lets it. Losing a lot takes away your mental toughness. When a player is not mentally tough, he gets tentative. Mental toughness allows a player to transform a negative situation into a positive one. Keep your mind in the game, and never lose your focus! Mental toughness allows you to eliminate and overcome psychological barriers.

Mental toughness is an attitude. It allows a player to keep going when others have given up. When a team is mentally tough, it wins the close games and the games it's supposed to win.

When a player is inconsistent, it's usually because of a lack of mental toughness. We often say the other team won the game because of luck. Instead, the other team was probably more mentally tough.

Mental toughness is the ability to quickly get over a mistake or adversity. It is also the ability to keep your intensity at a high level for a long period of time. If a player is afraid or has any doubts, he's probably going to lose. Mental toughness is the ability to battle your emotions. Mental toughness is when you're willing to face new challenges and not be intimidated by them.

Mental toughness is finding resolve regardless of the situation. A player has to be battle tested. He has to persevere and keep fighting. Mental toughness is about setting aside your distraction and focusing on your goals.

Mental toughness is remembering to always keep your head up during adversity. Mental toughness is gaining and maintaining a mental edge.

Size

It's not how big an athlete is. It's how big he plays. Big athletes tend to be uncoordinated. An athlete can make up for size with quickness and defensive intensity. Playing smart can also neutralize size. Use size as an asset, not a liability. People never notice how small an athlete is until he makes a mistake. It's not the size of the body. It's the size of the heart that counts. Numbers alone don't tell coaches about a player's heart. Success goes beyond the numbers. Desire makes a winner.

Complacency

Mediocrity and complacency have different names. However, if someone studies both attitudes, he will find that they are the same. Complacency is the silent killer and gives a false sense of security.

When a player becomes complacent, he doesn't adjust. He doesn't seek new opportunities or challenges. He becomes overconfident. A player has to realize that he can always work harder and achieve more goals. The perfect game should be his benchmark. A player can't recapture past glory or rest on laurels. He has to play every play like it's his last. A player can never afford to look past his next opponent.

For a great player, there's no such thing as a routine play. Great players play hard on every play. Complacent players are content just to get to the playoffs. They have no spirit or enthusiasm. They care more about stats than winning.

Complacency is when a player knows he is capable of reaching a certain level but never meets expectation or his full potential because he doesn't put forth the effort. Complacent players tend to believe the hype and bask in the glory of victory too long. Complacent players don't take advantage of their ability. A player can always grow, improve, and elevate his game to the next level. Complacency is when players come out flat and let the other team set the tempo. Complacency is when a player becomes a victim of his own success.

Complacency is part of human nature. There's no adrenaline rush. Don't ever relax. Keep your competitive spirit flowing. Don't let complacency become your friend. Complacency stops you from seizing the moment.

When a team becomes complacent, they play sloppy and undisciplined and don't pay attention to details in practice or the games. The players aren't mentally or physically prepared, and they aren't focused on team goals. During periods of complacency, a player becomes lazy, tired, and disinterested. He plays with no effort. The best way to combat complacency is to always keep a high energy level, especially during practice.

Defining a Career

His peers and history will judge a player. A career is made of goals, memories, and milestones.

Maturity

Maturity is making the sacrifices that are necessary in order to achieve your goals. Maturity is learning something new about yourself every day. When you mature, you will automatically set your goals and standards higher. Maturity is about learning how and what it takes to win. Mature players have the poise to exploit mistakes and mismatches. The more mature a player is, the more humble he becomes. Maturity is about keeping an even keel, not getting too high or too low.

Maturity is keeping things in perspective. Maturity is when the game slows down in your mind, your instincts improve, and you visualize everything. Maturity is understanding what got your team the lead and staying with that game plan. Maturity is not pointing fingers or making excuses.

Maturity is learning to respond to adversity and bad games. Maturity is learning to play more efficiently and smart. Part of the maturation process is becoming more focused and paying more attention to details. Maturity brings forth patience, and a player doesn't panic in pressure situations.

Consistency comes with maturity. With maturity, a player develops confidence and character. Maturity is when a player mentality begins to match the level of his talent. Maturity is the climax of a mental and physical transformation. Maturity is a player understanding the mental approach that he must have to be successful. During the maturation process, a player grows with each practice and game. Maturity allows a player to step up when his team needs him the most.

Playing with Pride

Every year, a coach should give his team a character test. Winning is mainly attitude and being prepared. Sometimes, you just have to follow your destiny and never take anything for granted. Every day, a player should play and practice with pride. Pride is a great motivator. Pride is confidence in your skills and ability. Playing with pride is about playing with obsessive determination, swagger, purpose, loyalty, and respect for the game.

Cherish every challenge! To be the best you have to compete against the best! You have to learn from the best. Finally, you have to beat the best. Being the best means never being satisfied. Dreams involve sacrifices. Don't watch someone else live out your dreams.

The Off-season

In the off-season, most players lose their intensity. A player should develop an off-season workout plan where he devotes several hours a day to studying game film and going through rigorous weightlifting. A player should use the off-season to set goals for the upcoming season. The off-season is when a player prepares mentally and physically for the challenges ahead. The off-season is a test of self-motivation. During the off-season, a team can find out who is truly committed.

Off-season workouts have a lot to do with late season success. A player needs endurance to stand the rigors of the entire season. Playoff dreams begin in the off-season.

There are three types of player energy:

- **Playing energy:** Be a catalyst; play physical
- **Motivational energy:** Be a leader
- **Mental energy:** Play with confidence

Team Leader

A leader has to have enough pride to come back from failure. He has to be a strong, aggressive motivator. A leader must bring energy to the team. A leader's teammates will feed off his energy. A leader doesn't let his team relax or become complacent. A leader finds the weak link on the team and motivates him to improve.

To be a leader, a player's teammates must respect his work ethic and attitude. A leader's love for the game will rub off on others. A leader sets a standard for everyone else to follow. A leader should not be moody and self-centered. A leader has to lead according to his own style. He can't copy someone else's style. A leader is a stabilizer in the locker room.

A team leader doesn't just tell teammates about a winning attitude. He shows them how to win. Leaders have to be seen and heard. Being a leader isn't about what you do or say, but it's how you do and say it. A leader transforms a group of guys into a team. A leader raises his game and takes his team to another level.

A team leader has to set the tempo on offense and defense and in practice. He brings energy and effort and makes plays when his team needs him the most. Leadership is about taking ownership. That ownership is called accountability. It's the job of the team leaders to make sure the team stays focused. Leadership is managing and developing personnel. Leadership is also managing personalities. One element of leadership is taking the pressure off everyone else and putting it on yourself.

A team leader must be tough, courageous, aggressive, and emotional. He must be a motivator. He must have a competitive urge and mental stamina. Many teams lack confidence because they don't have a team leader. When a team is on the cusp of defeat, the leader has to step forward. A leader takes responsibility for these actions. A leader doesn't let fear hold him back. A leader has boundless confidence. A team leader is an extension of the coach.

A team leader must be a tenacious competitor. As a leader, he must transcend his sense of urgency to his teammates. Because other people look to a leader for guidance, he can't suppress his emotions.

A team leader should come to spring training in shape and on time. He should lead by example and be a model citizen. A leader is a role model, whether he likes it or not, so he shouldn't do anything to embarrass his team, his family, or himself. When a team leader lowers his expectations, the followers will lower their expectations as well.

Leadership is a component of chemistry. In order for players to bond, they need a leader. A leader is a guy whom his teammates can count on in the clutch. A team leader keeps a positive attitude in the locker room.

Leadership

Leadership is the ability to take over a game with your decision-making.

Instincts

Instinct is mental awareness of everything going on around you. It is playing off adrenaline and reacting before you think. It is everything moving in slow motion. It requires concentration and intelligence. Instincts come from practice, repetition, and experience. It is a coach's mentality. It is insight and raw talent. Instinct is a natural feel for the game. It happens when you visualize the next play. It enables a player to take his game to the next level.

Playing on the Road

Winning on the road is difficult and rewarding. Players must be aggressive on the road and take the crowd out of the game. This can be done by getting an early lead. On the road, it is hostile territory, but the visiting team must play loose and free. The visiting team won't have some of the normal distractions that they usually encounter at home, such as dealing with hometown fans and getting tickets for friends. However, they will have to combat the fatigue from traveling.

Don't give up on the road! Coming back shows character! Score early on the road to calm your team and the crowd. Defense, a good bench, mental toughness, and veteran leadership are the keys to winning on the road. The physical condition of your team also determines getting wins on the road.

Championship Teams

Championship teams win at home and win half their road games. They win close games. They win in their division. They beat teams with losing records. They play aggressively and have sage and savvy veterans. They have a team leader. They practice hard and have a good work ethic. They take nothing for granted. They set a standard and have lofty goals. They have chemistry, along with pride and swagger. They have a good defense. They are consistent and fundamentally sound.

The players on a championship team have to be willing to pay the ultimate price, sacrificing their bodies on every play and every game. They are adding to and rewriting history. For one brief moment, their team is the best in the world. Remember how it feels! Years from now, they will still appreciate what their teams have accomplished.

Champions make big plays at the turning point of the game. Success one year doesn't parlay into success the next. However, good teams find ways to win. They peak at the right time.

Defense is the trademark of a championship team. A championship fills a void and validates everything.

Your dedication should know no limits. You can't rest on laurels. You have to have talent and resolve.

In order to be a champion, a team has to know how to win and have leadership and focus. A championship is your claim on history. Being a champion gives you a competitive edge. You've been there and won. After you win a championship, you will relive that moment for the rest of your life.

The champions will always be the team that best handles adversity. Championship teams are always ready to play and find ways to win. They know how to win in several different styles.

A championship defense plays unselfish with discipline, and they are very physical. The defense has to be the hunter. Championship teams take pride in their defense. Defense is about effort, and coaching and motivation can enhance that effort.

C: character
H: heart
A: ambition
M: maturity
P: poise

A Champion

When you climb the highest mountain
or swim across the greatest sea, when you
get to the other side, you'll find me.
R. E. Lee

Practice

Each practice should be a search for excellence. Perfect practice makes perfection! Practice is an art. Practice is preparation. The more a player practices, the fewer mental mistakes he will make.

The second unit must practice with the same intensity as the first. Hopefully, there isn't a big disparity in talent between the first and second unit. If you practice hard, the games will take care of themselves. The way a team practices carries over into the game. Being prepared is half of the battle. Fine-tuning your skills doesn't always mean changing stances or techniques. Practice is the foundation of success.

Practice against someone who is older, bigger, and stronger. Look at yourself, and say, "What can I do better?" Challenge your teammates to raise their level of play! Practice should have meaning. Practice with pride! At practice, there should be a sense of urgency.

Early in the season, practices should be long and hard. Practices should be just as tough as a regular season game. The coach should spend the majority of the practice time concentrating on defense. Toward the end of the season, a coach should cut down on practice time because fatigue is one of the main reasons for injuries.

Practice should be fast, aggressive, and detailed. After each practice and game, the coach has to grade each player on effort and production. Practice is gaining perfection through repetition. The only way to improve is with practice.

Success isn't guaranteed. That's why a player has to practice hard. When he's not practicing, someone else is. All talent has to be developed through practice. There will always be someone with more talent than you, but don't let them outwork you. A player has to trust the lessons that he has learned in practice. If a player is good, he can be elite with practice.

When it comes to practice, you get out of it what you put in it.

Practice Objectives

- Keep it simple.
- If you're not going to use it in the game, don't practice it.
- Use time efficiently.
- Practice fundamentals first and game situations next.
- Practice until the fundamentals become automatic.
- Practice in the position that you're going to play.
- Give yourself a grade after practice.
- Practice can teach endurance, but it can't teach hustle.
- Go full speed in practice; practice should be competitive.
- Start practice with warm-up drills.

Work Ethic

Work ethic shows that you want to be the best. It gives you control over your own destiny. A person gets out of something what you put into it. A good work ethic means you are dedicated to perfection. Work ethic demonstrates that you are a student of the game and committed to the game. Work ethic determines consistency. Work ethic is about closing the gap of where you are compared to where you want to be. Hard work eventually turns into confidence. Work ethic gives you the extra advantage necessary to put you in an elite category. A player makes dreams happen with work ethic. Working hard isn't the exception. It's the rule.

Stability

Having the same coach, the same players, and the same system is called stability. Stability brings success and inspires confidence! Stability is making long-term goals and commitment to the future.

There are no quick-fix solutions. Stable coaching staffs are usually successful. They have been together so long that they are able to make quick and accurate adjustments during the game. Changing coaches also slows down player development and team chemistry. Stability is about loyalty to and within an organization. The stability of an organization has a lot to do with the relationship between the owner, general manager, and coach.

Just like the organization, players also need a stable environment in order to succeed. That means that a player's role on his team shouldn't change from game to game.

Successful Organizations

Players and coaches don't win championships. Organizations do. The organization selects the players and coaches that best fit into its system. Success and commitment starts at the top and then trickles down. Players, coaches, and fans usually don't argue with success. It's no coincidence that certain organizations are synonymous with success. In good organizations, new players just want to add to the legacy and fit into the culture. Successful organizations have a direction and a commitment to winning. Every organization has to have a vision. Championships are won step by step.

It takes more than great players to win a championship. It also takes great coaches, general managers, and scouts. The efforts and hard work of an entire organization—not just one specific unit—contribute to winning championships.

Success is about work:
Doing your homework, teamwork and work ethic.
—R. E. Lee
Success is when your desire matches
or exceeds your ability.
—R. E. Lee

Defense

Defense is a team effort. A defense has to be respected and feared. Defense is about anticipation, not reacting. Defense is a mind-set. A defense has to create problems and turnovers and limit the offensive options. Give the other team many defensive looks to break their rhythm. The defense has to disrupt the offense and be the aggressor. Defense takes hard work and dedication. Intensity should personify the defense. A good defensive team is properly positioned. It has good footwork, depth, versatility, speed, and talent, and it is consistent.

Offense is about raw talent. Defense is about being a student of the game. Every good defense has many blue-collar players.

Teamwork

A team is a unified, unselfish group. A team is bonded together by a work ethic called *teamwork*. Teamwork is doing what's best for the team and being willing to help in whatever capacity necessary. Teamwork is about being accountable to each other. Teamwork is more than a cliché. Teamwork takes effort! The team must have a common agenda. Teamwork is a group of players acting as a collective unit. Teamwork is about having one state of mind and one goal.

Being a team player means a player who just wants to contribute. Teamwork is about respect and chemistry. A player has to play smart and put aside his ego. Showmanship fills the stadiums, but teamwork wins games. Every team needs someone to make sacrifices in order to be successful. Players must accept their individual and team responsibilities.

A team is several players coming together as one. A team has one mind, one body, and one agenda. Your teammates are your second family. There must be a trust and a bond among teammates. A team is a group of individuals coming together to accomplish one goal. Teams that win games toward the end of the season are the ones that have discipline, focus, chemistry, and good coaches.

Teamwork is knowing what your teammates are supposed to do and counting on them to do it. Teamwork is learning to appreciate the hard work and effort of your teammates. Everyone in the locker room must be committed to each other. The team concept is about accountability. As a coach, the only thing I ask from any team is a commitment to winning. A team is a family, and families are built on trust.

The teamwork concept builds character and trust. There must be one goal and one vision. Teamwork wins championships.

Coaching

Rating a coach includes the following criteria:

- recruiting/scouting
- the respect he gets from his players
- the ability to motivate
- winning percentage
- making adjustments during the game
- time management
- organization
- leadership
- teaching fundamentals, sportsmanship, and character

As a coach, winning the players' respect is winning half the battle. Players have to trust the coach's judgment. Getting players to be believe in what he says is the difference between success and failure as a coach. The first thing a coach has to do is come in and change attitudes and the culture. Players want to be motivated. A coach must mold a team in his own image. A coach must have an aura of toughness and passion.

Leadership starts at the top. Teams feed off the coach's emotions. A team's confidence starts with the coach. An intense coach will keep his team focused. The coach must know how to delegate authority and give his team a sense of direction. A good coach gives his team an emotional edge. A coach has to be fair but keep his standard high. A coach has to know talent management. Talent management covers everything from game situations to playing time and egos. A coach should emphasize academics as well as sportsmanship. The influence he will have on his players will last a lifetime.

Coaching is a special job. A coach has to be a father, teacher, and motivator. A coach has to be a good communicator. He has to know when to criticize a player and when to pat him on the back.

Coaches need to be great motivators. Being a great motivator is when the team believes what the coach is saying. In certain scenarios, a coach has to rely on past success and experience. If it worked before, try it again! Motivation is when a coach alters the mentality of a player in a positive way.

Coaching is a revolving door. Every coach replaces someone, and one day, someone will replace him. A coach has to have a resilient personality. A coach has to challenge his veteran players to step up and show leadership. It's the nature of the job that a coach will be second-guessed. Many coaches become victims of expectations.

The coach has to be the CEO. He leads and organizes everything. A good coach gets respect because of the credibility and trust that the players have for him. If you're a good coach, the players will respond to your leadership. The coach's main job is to get the ball in the hands of the playmakers. Great coaches always have great players. However, great coaches still find ways to make great players better, to have an impact on every game, and to utilize players in the roles that best fits them. As a coach, you have to know your team and be aware of their personalities and needs. As a coach, it isn't what you know. It's how much you're able to teach.

A good teacher doesn't force his philosophy on players. He helps the players excel in areas with things they do best and helps to fix areas in which they are weak. As a coach, your first job is to teach the players everything they need to succeed. Every player wants to learn, but a coach can't teach the love of the game. A coach's legacy is in the lives that he has touched and changed.

Effective Coaches

Players and organizations want proven winners. A coach must be positive and energetic. He must have a winning formula. He must have a well-prepared game plan and trust in it. He must be a shrewd judge of talent. He must find the right combination, integrate pieces, and link personalities. He must mold and nurture raw, young talent. A coach must properly utilize the bench when the situation dictates it. He has an orderly and direct approach.

He must be a teacher but don't overcoach. He must refuse to accept failure. He has to be flexible and can't treat every player the same. He has to know how his players react to pressure. He must pass on his standard and toughness to his players. The game plan should emphasize details.

The coach has the ability to adjust to situations and a new era. He teaches fundamentals, character, discipline, dedication, and teamwork. He has a powerful personality that brings stability to a team. He manages and deflates certain player egos. He changes the system or finds players to fit it. He keeps the team focused and instills confidence in the team.

He has a game plan that is simplified but not predictable. He is a motivator that finds new ways to generate enthusiasm. He bridges the generation gap. He doesn't adopt someone else's coaching style. He sets immediate goals and starts preparing for the next team the minute after the last game.

Character

Character can be traced back to your family. Character is a desire to do things the right way. It is the ability to turn something negative into something positive. Character is doing what is right even when it's unpopular. Character helps you make informed decisions. It determines who you are and what your fate in life is. Character is developed early in life. Character is about inner fortitude. Lack of character will limit how far you can go in life.

Character is learning to make the best of a bad situation. Stature doesn't make the man. Character makes the man. A person who compromises his values or principles has no character. A person has to live within certain restraints, the boundaries of morality. Without character, your self-esteem and demeanor will erode.

Players and coaches can't lead without character. Don't compromise your integrity. If a player lives for the moment, those situations will always let them down. Character starts at home with your parents. Your character is developed from the values that your parents have instilled in you. It's hard to consistently win without character. One bad attitude can upset the cohesiveness of the entire team.

Sports

Sports have transcended over into our culture. America is about competition. We are obsessed and motivated by competition. Competition makes an athlete a better player and person.

Sports build an athlete's self-esteem. Sports help to improve a person's social acceptance. Sports allow us to embrace our competitive spirit. Winning gives a player a sense of accomplishment. Sports teach teamwork and sportsmanship. Sports allow us to express our personalities.

Training Regimen

Your training regimen should include weightlifting, studying film, exercising, running, taking vitamins, and eating a low-fat diet. Your training can't be sporadic. Training has a lot to do with your consistency. A good training regimen will mold you into a complete player. Your training regimen will make you resilient and mentally tough and sets your attitude for the upcoming season.

Your legs are the most important part of an athlete's body. Your legs provide balance, power, and endurance. If you come to training camp out of shape, you'll be a step behind everyone else for the rest of the season.

Successful Teams

Successful teams don't confuse entertainment with skills and talent. Showmanship can be used to complement talent but not replace it. Good teams find ways to take advantage of the other team's mental mistakes. Fundamentals win games at every level of competition.

Every team needs a tandem to be successful. The tandem should include a great player and a player that will be great one day. The great player can be used as a mentor to the younger player that will eventually fill his role.

In a complete season, you're going to have peaks and valleys. Losing streaks begin when you lose your mental focus. A mental breakdown always shows up on the defense first. The best way to keep your mental focus is to practice often and take practice seriously.

Dedication

Winning has a price. It's called dedication. Passion for the game is born out of dedication. Passion for the game is when you appreciate the opportunities that you have been given and you take nothing for granted. Dedication is a combination of hard work and effort.

Dedication is when you constantly hone your skills. Dedication is when there is strong determination to progress toward excellence. Dedication is about staying focused on your objectives. Dedication is a tireless and relentless pursuit of a task. Dedication is about earning the right to win and having the desire for perfection. Dedication is accomplishing your goals through hard work. Dedication is giving the maximum effort.

Fatigue

When you're fatigued, the body doesn't react as quickly to the signals from your brain. When you're tired, your feet and hands stop responding or respond slower. A player starts reaching and stops using his footwork. When you're tired, it shows up in your defense first. Fatigue is the cause of the silliest fouls and penalties. Turnovers are another sign of fatigue. Late-in-the-game fatigue throws off your timing. In order to win the battle against fatigue, you can't let it affect you mentally. When a player is fatigued, he has to play off emotions.

Intangibles

The intangibles means doing whatever it takes to win. It goes beyond the numbers. It is about playing above your ability. Intangibles often go unnoticed, but they are just as important as talent. The intangibles are things like character, heart, courage, confidence, dedication, commitment, chemistry, sacrifice, teamwork, leadership, poise, playing hurt, attitude, instincts, game management skills, and work ethic. Intangibles are the subtle qualities that make certain players great. Intangible are the things that you can't coach or measure.

Patience

Patience is mental discipline. Patience allows a player to rest and regroup. It is a lot easier to slow down the tempo than speed it up. That's why the early portion of the game is so important. Patience will negate speed and size. Not being patient will cause a team to miss out on opportunities. Lack of experience and not being patient usually shows up at the beginning of the game. When patient, a player relaxes, stays focused, and does what he has to do in order to win. Patience is the ability to handle the growing pains of youth and having grace under pressure.

Playing Physical

Playing physical means denying and beating opponents to the spot where he wants to go. Playing physical is about being aggressive, playing with heart, and throwing around your body. When a team is playing physical, they are penetrating and attacking. Physical players like to mix it up. They don't mind getting cut, bruised, or bloody. Give up your body. Go shoulder-to-shoulder and head-to-head with your opponent! Playing physical is creating space where there is no space. When a team plays physical, they put fear in their opponents. If a team is not playing physical, they're not playing the game right. Physical teams are more consistent than finesse teams.

Playing physical is about sacrificing your body. Playing physical is when your intensity forces the other team to make mistakes. You impose your will on your opponent. You make your presence felt, dictate the tempo of the game, and force turnovers. After a team loses a game, they need to establish a physical presence early in the next game. Playing physical keeps the other team off balance.

Pressure

Expectation means pressure. There's a sense of urgency. Nobody is immune to pressure. Pressure is when a person realizes that he might fail. Pressure is self-inflicted. Pressure will either turn into stress or motivation. Pressure can cause a player to lose focus.

Repeat to yourself before every game, "I love pressure." Don't relax but feel comfortable! Play with confidence, hope, and poise! When you're under pressure, you must believe in your ability. You have to challenge yourself in order to become a better player.

Fear

An athlete can't be afraid to fail. Fear comes from a lack of confidence. It's not trusting your ability. Fear is not being prepared for adversity. Adversity will only make you stronger and better. To combat fear, don't think too hard. Just let your instincts take over. It's a difference between being nervous and being afraid. In a big game, it's okay to be nervous.

Killer Instinct

The pendulum has swung. Today, defense is the name of the game. After a win, take that emotion into the next game. If you get tentative with a lead, you'll let the other team back into the game. Don't just try to win. Make a statement, and send a message. The atmosphere has to stay the same. There's no margin for error. A team has to keep the intensity and its competitive spirit throughout the game. Show your opponent no mercy! Give them something to remember in the rematch! Finish them off properly! Take away your opponent's confidence! Destroy everyone in your path to victory and close his window of opportunity. Create a legacy with total domination.

When you have the lead, you control your own destiny. You want to take the life out of the other team. Put pressure on your opponent to force them into mistakes. Don't let them have a rally. Veteran players know how to close out a game. Veteran teams always have that killer instinct.

Your team has to stop your opponent's will to win and set the tempo. You must take out an underdog quickly. When the other team gains momentum, your team has to answer with a score. Keep that emotional edge! Scoring early sets the tempo so your team can finish off the opponent in style. You have to take advantage of breaks. Don't play the scoreboard. Play the other team!

Don't become complacent! Control the environment and the momentum! Show your opponent that you mean business. Most young teams don't have killer instinct because they lose focus. A team with killer instinct plays offense and defense for the entire game without a lapse in concentration. Your team must have that seek-and-destroy mentality and realize that no lead is safe.

Controlling the end of the game is about tempo and conditioning. Killer instincts are about getting stronger as the game goes on. Killer instincts are the ability to seal the deal. Championship teams have killer instincts.

Camaraderie

Camaraderie is when teammates rally around each other. There's an unbreakable chemistry en route to a single mission or purpose. There's a sense of togetherness. There's no individual glory. The team concept comes first! Everyone has the same mind-set, and everyone relies on each other. Camaraderie is about being a focused and committed group. Camaraderie is diversity mixed together well. Camaraderie is when a team becomes a family. Camaraderie is harmony that develops naturally. Camaraderie is learning to trust one another. It is when adversity doesn't divide a team but brings them closer. Team unity promotes valor, high energy, and emotion. We win and lose together. We laugh and cry together. We are a team.

Underachievers

Underachievers have a bevy of talent but lack character, discipline, vision, passion, work ethic, and mental toughness. In order to be a winner, a player has to be obsessed with winning and motivated by perfection. When underachievers fail, they often blame others.

Underachievers lack confidence! They don't use their resources wisely. Underachievers never fulfill their commitments, and they are constantly making excuses and mistakes.

Momentum

Momentum is when the intensity increases in your favor and every play is critical. Momentum is a shift in confidence with the ability to seize the moment. Momentum is short and can turn around on a team quickly. Momentum is when all cylinders are clicking. Momentum often shifts with a turnover or back-to-back scores. Momentum allows a team to dictate its styles. Momentum feeds off emotion. Momentum is building on something positive.

Teams want to grab the momentum early so they can control the tempo of the game. The team should keep the emotions and its energy going. Momentum is real. It's not just a cliché. If the team's opponent takes the momentum, the other team has to seize it back. History only respects winners.

Sports Purist

A sports purist cherishes tradition, respecting and remembering what the game used to be like. Purist-like players emphasize fundamentals, character, and sportsmanship. A purist believes how players win is just as important as winning and dedication is just as important as stats. A purist is like those blue-collar players who give 100 percent in victory and defeat. A purist loves those unsung heroes who feel personal success comes from team success.

The fundamentals are knowing the basics, having discipline within the scheme, and being mechanically sound. Fundamentals include knowing the general rules of the game; having eye and hand coordination, proper footwork, and instincts; and executing the game plan.

Effort

Effort is a combination of determination, strength, and agility. Effort is about being focused, having keen knowledge and precise standards, and wisely using your resources to produce maximum output. The losses that hurt the most are the ones where players don't give their best effort, when the other team just outplays them. The losses that occur when your opponent just wanted the victory more are demoralizing. Effort is the key to achieving all your goals.

Effort starts in practice. Effort is trying harder and getting better. Effort is about maintaining a high energy level. A coach can't teach effort. Effort is the difference between being good and being great. Keep pushing forward and striving for greatness. Effort takes no talent. Effort is about heart. If you work hard, everything else will come easy. If you give every fiber you have in your body toward obtaining a victory, you'll have no regrets.

Effort is contagious. It spreads from one player to the next. Effort is giving more than the bare minimum. Older players have to push younger players in practice and games. Older players give the younger players someone to lean on and talk to. Effort is preparing hard, working hard, and playing hard. You never know which play will lose a game so you have to play your hardest on every play. A player has to try to make and finish every play! A player has to give 100 percent all the time.

Attitude

The most important word in the English language is *attitude*. Always practice the power of the mind. Nothing on earth is stronger than willpower. Many things contribute to your destiny. However, your attitude puts you in control of your destiny. Playing physical is about attitude. Attitude determines work ethic. Attitude gives you an edge. Most games are won from the neck up, that is, with attitude.

What separates a winner from a loser? The will to win! Everyone wants to win, but few are committed to winning. The more you win, the more you understand what it takes to win.

Winning builds unity and pride. Winning is a choice. You can reinforce that choice with hard work and dedication. If you lower your expectations, you'll never know your potential.

Be obsessed with one goal, the will to win. Make winning a habit. Winning is everything! There is no plan B. Somebody's will has to be broken. The will to win isn't about how much ability you have, but it's what you do with it. It's not about who you are playing. It's about your competitive fire.

Self-Discipline

A commitment starts with self-discipline and is followed up with action. I remain confident and never become complacent. I approach sports with the same vigor I approach everything else in life. I live and play by an oath to give my all on every play. I won't let excuses delay my success.

Rivalry

A rivalry is more than just another formidable opponent. A rivalry is about survival. A rivalry is a war. The coaches can throw out the stats and records. It is important to know a team can win in a playoff-like atmosphere. In a rivalry, it is important that the players don't get caught up too much in the emotional aspect of the game because there is little margin for error in a rivalry contest. A rivalry is about inspiring each other to new heights. A true rivalry never loses its luster.

A rivalry is usually two division teams vying for the same title. Friendly local competition and tradition usually start rivalries. When a team has a proud tradition, it will have many rivals. In a rivalry game, a team can't let the excitement cause it to lose its focus.

Rookies

Rookies are on the team to add depth. Few start immediately. Rookies should know and accept their role. Rookies spend most of their time learning a system, adjusting to a new environment, and gaining confidence. The most important thing is to be ready when called upon and stay in the flow of the game. A rookie should do whatever is good for the team concept and practice the fundamentals every day. Always stay mentally and physically ready to play! For a rookie, ability alone is not enough. A player needs maturity to grow.

If a coach treats a rookie like a rookie, he will act and play like one. As a rookie, a player needs to show potential. If the season starts slow for a first-year player, he can't get down. He has to just keep working hard. He has to let the game come to him.

Rookies are judged on three things: talent, ability to execute, and attitude. Rookies must pay attention to details and come out ready to play. A rookie's first year will be a test in fortitude. As a rookie, trying to get off to a quick start can be counterproductive.

Most rookies don't lack knowledge. They just lack experience. Every rookie must rise to the challenge.

Rookies usually have trouble on the defensive side of the ball because they're learning to adjust to game tempo. Rookies have to establish a daily routine on and off the field. Rookies aren't expected to play flawless. All rookies will experience growing pains.

Rookies have to learn to harness their energy and play under control. Coaches sometimes delay starting a rookie to reduce the pressure and expectations. As a rookie, it's important to try to eliminate the distractions and stay focused.

A Go-To Guy

A go-to guy makes things happen. He is a big playmaker and has supreme confidence. He is a team leader and a coach on the field. He always expects to play at a high level. He is consistent. He understands pressure. He is usually a veteran. He has the ability to change the tempo of the game. He can turn it on and off when he wants to.

Never Forget the Ten Ds

- Discipline: set goals
- Desire: work ethic
- Dedication: commitment
- Domination: killer instincts
- Destiny: must be fulfilled
- Demand: excellences
- Demeanor: your mentality
- Defense: physical
- Development: reaching your potential
- Defeat: avoid it; remember what it feels like

Intensity

Intensity is controlled aggression. Intensity is energy in motion. Not only does a player want to beat his opponent, he wants to mentally and physically wear them down. He does this with intensity.

Intensity is a high energy level. Intensity is pure, raw emotion. A team can't win without it. Intensity usually can be measured with desire. The more desire a play has, the more intense he will become. If a player paces himself, he's cheating his teammates. Teams that play with a lot of intensity must have plenty of depth. Intensity starts at practice and carries over into the game. Intensity gives a player an edge over his opponent.

Intensity has to be in your DNA. You can't teach it. A coach can measure a player's intensity by the way he plays defense.

Consistency

As an athlete, everybody has one moment in time. Consistency will be his greatest test. Consistency is regularly performing up to expectations. Consistency is very little variance in performance. Consistency is maintaining a level of excellence. Consistency is being fundamentally sound and not making mental mistakes. Consistency comes from experience, mental toughness, attitude, discipline, maturity, practice, work ethic, and the ability to be focused. Consistency is the difference between being a contender or a pretender.

In a short playoff series, the team that is the most consistent will win. In order for some young players to be consistent, they must get more playing time.

A player has to be consistent. He has to remember what his role is and what he does best. Play to your strengths, and focus on attention to details. Consistency is the ability to play well on the road, under pressure, and in the spotlight. The difference between being good and being great is consistency. Be consistent with who and what you are. Every practice, every drill, every play, and every game is important.

Role Player

A role player is a player with limited ability, but he has great spirit and determination. A role player brings energy off the bench. A role player should do what he is capable of doing, nothing more and nothing less. Every role is important.

Role players make an average team good and a good team better. Veteran players are more willing to accept the position of role player. Players coming off the bench must be consistent and know their job description and their responsibilities.

Role players must have many subtle qualities. They are invaluable. Role players are just as important to a team as the starters. Role players have to be unselfish team players. Role players are what I call the *X-factor*.

Role players have to come in the game and make an immediate impact. Role players need to have the same mentality and objectives as a starter. The coach has to have confidence in his role players. Role players usually play better at home than on the road. A role player has to mentally accept his role.

Role players are traditionally hard workers. Role players make sacrifices to benefit the team. The negative side of being a role player is that a young player can be labeled as a role player and never expand his game. Role players fill weak spots on the roster and provide the team with an emotional lift.

A role player is the missing ingredient, an unsung hero. Role players give a team balance. Good role players are always in the right place at the right time. Role players are a critical element of any winning team. Furthermore, role players are more likely to accept their role on a winning team.

Role players have to embrace their secondary roles. Their main job is to be ready and prepared and to bring energy. Role players must play within themselves and within the framework of the offense. A role player shouldn't try to do too much or try to win the game on one play.

A role player should:

- Have the intangibles
- Blend in with the starters
- Understand the game and the game plan
- Be a hustler and a scraper (come off the bench aggressively)

- Bring energy to the team (come in and make something happen)
- Be skilled at several positions
- Be a hardworking overachiever

Veteran Players

There is no substitute for experience. With experience and leadership comes accountability. What matters the most about experience is to have big game and playoff experience. It is imperative that playoff-caliber teams have veteran players who have been there before and can get the job done. Veteran players can teach younger players how to win and teach the team about the fundamentals of the game. Experience helps build character. Experience allows a player to lead by example. Veteran players are unselfish and don't have big egos.

Young players often play down to the level of their competition. Veteran players are resilient and able to bounce back from a huge deficit. Veteran players know what the coach expects, and they usually deliver. Veteran players do the little things, and they play smart. Veteran players grind it out, and they concede nothing.

A veteran team will outhustle and outthink a young team. Veteran players have to redefine their roles using wisdom to compensate for declining physical ability. Experience wins more close games than talent. Experience offers valuable insight that a player can't get anywhere else.

Veteran players know how to lead. They know how to prepare and make adjustments. Longevity is about heart and work ethic, not just talent. While the younger players are getting comfortable with the speed of the game and developing their instincts, the veteran players have to embrace the younger players in order for it to be a perfect blend. It takes time for players to trust and believe in each other.

Determination

Determination is when you won't be denied. It is putting forth all your energy and learning to overcome adversity. Determination is the inner strength and willpower to complete a task.

Poise

Poise is good game management skills and decisions. Poise is when a player mentally understands the situation. Poise is playing loose but with discipline. Poise allows a player to execute and respond when he's under pressure. Poise helps a player to elevate his game to the next level. Poise allows a player to dictate the pace of the game. Poise is controlling your emotions. Poise is the charisma and confidence to finish a task. If a player loses his poise, he can't perform well.

Poise is the discipline to wait on opportunities. Poise is settling down and getting into the rhythm of the game. Keeping your composure means not making the moment bigger than it is. Poise means that a player doesn't panic in pressure situations.

Being Humble

Being humble is not bragging, having a calm demeanor without being complacent, or constantly making excuses. Being humble is when substance and sportsmanship prevails over style. Being humble is when you're happy with yourself and you respect others. Moreover, humility is setting aside your personal agendas.

Being humble is realizing an opponent can beat you on any given day. Being humble is when you realize nothing is promised to you. Being humble is about constantly wanting to grow, learn, and get better.

A High Sports IQ

If a player doesn't get angry about losing, some desire is missing. A player can get angry and still be in control. It is called leadership. Defeat will humble anybody. A lesson can be learned from each loss. An improved sports IQ comes from the frustration of losing.

A Blue-Collar Player

A blue-collar player has a strong work ethic. He is a role player. He does the intangibles. He is a hustler and has intensity. He is willing to play hurt. He doesn't crave the spotlight and plays for the love of the game and with passion.

Rebuilding

Because of free agency, more teams have to rebuild quickly and often. Rebuilding starts with attitude. Rebuild the spirit of the team by conditioning the mind and body. An organization wants players that believe in the system and they can teach them to win. A rebuilt team shouldn't just hope to win. They should believe that they can win. It is all about confidence.

An organization should keep the nucleus of the team intact when rebuilding. The purpose of rebuilding is to put a competitive team on the field. During rebuilding, some teams will need a complete overhaul. There are always calculated risks in rebuilding. There will be more questions than answers.

Rebuilding is about restoring order, talent, confidence, and tradition to a franchise. The two biggest problems in rebuilding are finding a young team leader and developing team chemistry. The team has to find an identity. The goal of rebuilding is to take another step forward each year. When an organization rebuilds, they trade experience for youth. Rebuilding is painful and unpredictable. It is not the speed but the quality of the rebuilding process that is important.

Remember that sports is a business. Teams rebuild because of financial reasons or the nucleus of the team is getting old. Some veterans should be kept to help develop some of the younger players and to make sure the rebuilding transition goes smoothly. Organizations have to be committed to rebuilding. The rebuilding process is often long and tedious.

When rebuilding, an organization will be maligned and have to face the wrath of the fans. Teams have to rebuild because so many teams have been dismantled through free agency. A team should never start rebuilding in the middle of the season. Rebuilding is an inevitable cycle. When rebuilding, a team has to draft a young star and find a strong supporting cast. The infusion of youth will cause many growing pains. In a stable organization, rebuilding is quicker and more successful.

Recruiting

When recruiting a player, the coach wants to know if the player is coachable. Does the player listen? Does the player take advice? What is the player's upside?

Recruiters must be honest and direct. Don't make guarantees! The recruiter must earn the player's respect and trust. Recruit for immediate needs. When a coach meets a recruit in person, he wants to find out the intangible things that he couldn't see on the films.

The coach should know a player's background and his reputation. The coach should know what type of home and environment the player came from, and he should be aware of any problems the player has had in the past—personal or academic—or any injuries.

Each player is an extension and representative of the program. The coach is looking for great players with potential leadership ability and a lot of enthusiasm. Raw talent is unpredictable. The recruiting process and their own popularity have spoiled players. If a player goes to a good team, it takes the pressure off him to be an immediate superstar. Everyone wants to be associated with a winner. Recruiting is where a team's foundation for success starts.

A Slump

A slump is a long drought or period of inconsistency. Sometimes there is no explanation or cure. A slump is unavoidable. A slump is when things that naturally happen no longer occur. Play out the slump and be patient! Don't try to change everything or be overly aggressive! When a player starts pressing, he gets out of rhythm, and this will prolong the slump.

Don't think or talk about the slump! A slump will start to play on the mind. When a player is in a slump, he has to continue to work hard, rely on being fundamentally sound, and think positive.

Playing with Heart

Take every game personal! It's not about revenge. It's about respect. Predictions are based on logic. Victories are based on desire. Playing with heart is about operating under adverse conditions. Playing with heart allows a player to overcome physical limitations. Playing with heart is about working harder and outhustling your opponent. Playing with heart is giving your best performance with the game on the line and being committed to succeeding on every play.

Seek that which is in your heart, and
everything else will follow.
R. E. Lee

Great Players

Great players are consistent. They have a tremendous amount of confidence and make the players around them better. They are humble warriors. They have good anticipation and possess grace under pressure.

All great players are born with the will to win. The will to win isn't about strength, weakness, athletic ability, or fatigue. It's about heart. The will to win is the knowledge of what it takes to win and striving for greatness.

Greatness

Is greatness determined by stats, individual awards, or championships? All great players have similar traits. Great players are mature and versatile. In order to be great, a player has to be durable. He has to be able to withstand the test of time. Great players do things that coaches can't teach. In the era of a specialist, the complete player is disappearing. When a player is great, the only person he has to prove something to is himself.

Great players make the impossible seem possible. Greatness just doesn't happen. It comes through practice and hard work. Great players like the big game atmosphere. A player should try to be good before he tries to be great. The word *great* is overused. How a player performs in big games defines his career. Great players are able to make quick adjustments and find weaknesses in their opponents. Greatness is sustained excellence. Great players leave an indelible mark on his teammates and the game. Greatness is when other players are compared to you.

Are you committed to being great? Greatness is a combination of motivation, skills, and will. Greatness is inside of you. Don't think about how good you are. Think about how great you can be. If you want to be great, there is no off-season. Know the expectations, and exceed them! You don't measure greatness. Let greatness measure you.

Swagger

Swagger is inner confidence. A team acts and talks like it is going to beat its opponent. Then it goes out and beats them. Swagger is walking with pride. Swagger is having the mystique of a champion.

Swagger is a championship team asserting itself early in the game. Winning creates positive energy. Swagger is the energy that comes from the love of the game.

A team must have the heart and attitude of a champ. When you're a team of destiny, you play with a certain swagger. Swagger is alertness, awareness, and resiliency. It's that won't-be-denied attitude!

Swagger isn't thinking that you're good. Swagger is knowing that you are good.

When It's Time to Retire

It's time to retire when the ability, commitment, and passion are no longer there. As players get older, it gets harder to mentally and physically prepare for a game. The love of the game includes passion, knowledge, and commitment. A player knows when his skills and love for the game are starting to diminish.

Perseverance

Perseverance is a lesson in faith and withstanding the test of time. Perseverance is about staying focused and never losing your confidence. Perseverance is about physical and mental stamina. Perseverance is the ability to endure times when things get worse before they get better. When one journey ends, another must begin!

Speed

Speed and quickness will stretch a defense. Speed and quickness translate into aggressiveness. To be effective, a player needs patience to go along with this speed. Speed can get a player in and out of trouble. Speed helps a player to overcome mistakes. Team speed can be the difference between winning and losing a close game. When a player is small, he needs to be multidimensional. Speed allows this to happen. Speed can be used in many ways. Speed on defense disrupts an offensive scheme. Speed wears down the opponent mentally. Speed allows a team to control the tempo. Speed is the equalizer.

The Draft

In the draft, a team wants to pick a player who comes in and makes an immediate impact. Raw talent is unpredictable. In the first round, a team wants to fill a need. After the first round, a team should take the best available player.

A team has to prepare for the draft like they are preparing for a championship. Drafting is like filling all the missing pieces to a puzzle. A team must draft for quality and depth. Scouts are mainly looking for the things that a player can't be taught, like the intangibles, speed, size, and instincts. The draft is based on potential, and there are no guarantees.

What Happens During a Winning Streak

During a winning streak, there is a development of trust and maturity, and role players elevate their games to another level.

Culture

The culture of an organization is a tradition that has been taught. The culture is a secondary environment created by the organization for the players. The culture must be one of stability and a consistent philosophy. The culture and mind-set of an organization starts at the top. A team has to believe in a winning tradition in order to succeed. The organization must search for players that have high values and high character. Everyone has to be on the same page and be fully committed. The organization should only acquire players that fit the team's culture.

Give your best. Then give a little more. Winning should be more than a relief. Winning should be fun.

Success is a process. You have to believe in the process. Winners set goals, work hard, and make improvements. Losers make excuses.

Winners

Winners are always multitasking. It doesn't matter that you play the game with passion and spirit. You must also play with focus and mental toughness. You should always expect to win, and nothing should change your expectations. Winning is more than a result. It's a mentality and a lifestyle, sometimes known as swagger. A player has to embrace winning and have fun.

Winning DNA

Winning DNA is to possess pure passion with no tolerance for losing and never accepting mediocrity.

Losers

The criterion of a loser is selfishness. He can't get rid of that habit quickly. He will have relapses. When a loser falls back into his selfish ways, he will need a mentor to constantly provide reinforcement and remind him to change back.

Passion

Passion is playing hard every day on every play. Before drafting a player, ask yourself, "Does that player have the passion for the game in his eyes?" Playing with a high motor is playing with passion. A coach can't measure emotion. Passion is playing for the love of the game, not for money or fame. Passion is focusing all your energy on winning. Passion helps to compensate for a lack of size. Passion for the game allows a player to overcome adversity and hard times. Always play with passion. Every game is meaningful, regardless of your opponent's record.

Mentor

A mentor is a role model. A mentor leads by example. A mentor is a born leader and teacher. The job of a mentor is to be a motivator. A mentor shows others the right pathway to take.

In order to be mentored, a player has to humble himself. A mentor helps to get younger players acclimated to the league. They provide counseling, discipline, and a controlled environment to younger players. They have been entrusted to guide others in the right directions. The mentor should have a vision for his students. A mentor helps the youth gain confidence and maturity. A mentor teaches the young players how to study game plans and prepare for the next game.

A Star

A star is a player who makes an immediate impact. Stars love the big games and the big stage. They excel in clutch situations. A star plays at a different level than everyone else. A star believes no one and nothing can stop him. A star is a player that's a difference maker. A star handles multiple roles every game. Stars play with a certain swagger. A star has the natural ability to move freely, purely, and gracefully. They make playing sports look easy.

A Closer

A closer has a calm demeanor under pressure, and he is a born leader. A closer has to assume his role, and he has to be comfortable as a closer. A coach can't appoint a closer. A closer takes on his role naturally. A closer is a clutch performer in big games. A closer embraces the moment. No system will work without a closer. At the end of the game, a closer has to say to himself, "This is my time."

Champions have vitamin H, Heart.

R. E. Lee

Life and sports are both about crossing the finish line. Start fast, and finish strong!

A motto for every game: Play hard, play with passion, and have fun!

Sense of Urgency

Run every play with a fast tempo. There's no time to relax. There is a sense of urgency when everything comes down to one moment or one play. Moreover, there is a sense of urgency when the window of opportunity is about to close.

When a team is in a must-win or winner-take-all situation, there must be a sense of urgency. In these games, if a team doesn't win, its season is over. Also, a sense of urgency is needed in a game where a team has to play its best in order to win. They must execute at a high level. A sense of urgency starts at practice. That's why a player must always run at practice and never walk.

Start Fast

It's imperative that a team get off to a great start. It allows a team to focus on its strengths and exploit the weakness of the defense. In order to get off to a fast start, a team has to be mentally ready to play. To avoid a slow start, a team has to find its energy, spirit, and competitive fire from the very beginning.

Final Notes

A player has to be confident enough to believe that he is supposed to be the best. Confidence is believing that dreams come true. Perseverance is believing that hard work pays off. Motivation is anything that inspires confidence. Motivational techniques have to be unique and creative.

Staying focused is not worrying about things you can't control. Underachievers are uninspired. Complacency is lack of effort. Poise is emotional control. A leader doesn't ask anything of his teammates that he doesn't do himself.

The key to being consistent is staying focused. Practice and work hard. In order for rookies to get more playing time, they must improve their defense. A team can't win in the playoffs without a leader. Rivalry games cause teams to get more focused.

Sooner or later, rookies are going to play like rookies. The rebuilding plan takes about three years. Poise is playing within yourself. Maturity is emotional stability. Coaches have to be humble and have mental stamina. Pressure is when others always expect you to win. Confidence is playing off your instincts.

Teams mold themselves around a leader. A leader keeps a team focused. Being humble is not letting the pressure and expectations get you down. Overachievers don't waste talent or potential and are constantly looking for ways to improve.

Dedication is a full commitment to something. Great players are self-motivators. Efficient execution demoralizes a defense. Excellence is maximizing your potential. If a player doesn't know the offense very well, he will play tentative.

The season isn't about winning streaks. A team just wants to get better each game. Chemistry is a group of guys who play well together that are passionate about the game. Having faith means being committed. On every play, a player has to be committed to winning.

Selfishness causes unneeded distractions. Attention to details means doing the little things. Close games are won because of maturity, discipline, mental toughness, good coaching and solid defense.

As the season goes on, the team should develop more chemistry. There are no shortcuts. Everyone is accountable for the way he plays and practices.

Playing with swagger is playing with confidence, having fun, and trusting each other.

Intelligent and mature teams don't panic. Coaches have to evolve with the times. Team means that it's not about you. It's about us.

About the Author

Reginald Lee has an MBA from Georgia Southern University. He has written several books and has a passion for playing and coaching sports. He currently resides in Jesup, Georgia, with his wife, Renee. They have four kids: Taylor, Perris, Eric, and Isaiah. He dedicates this book to his wife and kids.

Printed in the United States
By Bookmasters